Contents

Background Reading

Roommates

Sue Leather and Julian Thomlinson

Series Editor: Rob Waring
Story Editor: Julian Thomlinson
Series Development Editor: Sue Leather

HEINLE

Australia • Bra   • United States

HEINLE
CENGAGE Learning™

Page Turners Reading Library

Roommates

Sue Leather and Julian Thomlinson

Publisher: Andrew Robinson

Executive Editor: Sean Bermingham

Senior Development Editor:
Derek Mackrell

Assistant Editor: Sarah Tan

Director of Global Marketing:
Ian Martin

Content Project Manager:
Tan Jin Hock

Print Buyer:
Susan Spencer

Layout Design and Illustrations:
Redbean Design Pte Ltd

Cover Illustration: Eric Foenander

Photo Credits:
41 Adam Tinney/Shutterstock
42 Jaimie Duplass/Shutterstock
43 caracterdesign/iStockphoto
44 aabejon/iStockphoto

ISBN-13: 978-1-4240-4897-7
ISBN-10: 1-4240-4897-4

Heinle
20 Channel Center Street
Boston, Massachusetts 02210
USA

Cengage Learning is a leading provider of customized learning solutions with office locations around the globe, including Singapore, the United Kingdom, Australia, Mexico, Brazil, and Japan. Locate your local office at:
international.cengage.com/region

Cengage Learning products are represented in Canada by Nelson Education, Ltd.

Visit Heinle online at **elt.heinle.com**

Visit our corporate website at
www.cengage.com

Printed in the United States of America
1 2 3 4 5 6 7 – 14 13 12 11 10

People in the story

Bobby Harris
Bobby is a business student at Brenton. He is going to college for the first time.

Ash Browning
Ash is Bobby's roommate at Brenton College. He is also a business student.

Gloria Harris
Gloria is Bobby's mother.

Marvin Harris
Marvin is Bobby's father.

Jenny Basola
Jenny is an anthropology student. She is Ash and Bobby's friend.

Gayle King
Gayle is manager of the college cafeteria and Bobby's boss.

This story is set in Brenton, a college town in the northwestern United States.

Chapter 1

A big day

"Mom, please let me go," Bobby says.

Bobby is in front of his house with his mother and father. His bags are all in the car next to him. His mother looks worried.

"Just be sure to drive slowly, Bobby," Gloria Harris says to her son. "There are always a lot of cars on that highway from Powell to Brenton."

"Oh, Mom!" says Bobby. "It's OK." Bobby is driving to Brenton College for the first time and he can see that his mother is worried. *She's always worried about something,* he thinks.

But Bobby's worried, too, and his eyes are big behind his round glasses. He's worried about college, about a million different things. His mom and dad don't have a lot of money. Bobby knows that he has to work when he gets there. He has a job in the college cafeteria. Then there are his business studies. Bobby's worried about them, too. College is different from school. *Can I do well there?* he thinks. He'll live away from home, too, in the dorm—in a room with another student at the college. Most of all, Bobby's worried about his roommate. *I hope he's nice,* he thinks.

For the third or fourth time that Sunday morning, Bobby's mother says, "Remember to work hard at Brenton, Bobby. Remember that this is a big thing, going to college. You're the first in our family . . ."

"I have to go, Mom," Bobby says.

"Now, Gloria," says Bobby's dad, Marvin, smiling, "Bobby always works hard—you know that." Then he looks at Bobby. "But your mother's right, son. This is a big day for you."

"It's a big day," his mother says again. "Now, do you have everything? Are you sure?"

"Yes, I have everything!" Bobby says.

"Yes, he has everything, Gloria," says Bobby's dad.

"Come on," says Bobby's mother. "Take a photo of us all before you go. Then you can put it in your room at college."

"Oh, Mom, I have to go!" Bobby starts. But his mother goes into the house to look for the camera.

◇◇◇

Thirty minutes later, Bobby drives away from his parents' house. He looks back and sees his mom and dad at the door. His mother is crying, her face in his dad's shirt. Bobby wants to cry too, but he tries not to. He drives to the end of Willow Street, where the Harris family lives. Then he drives onto the road to Brenton.

It's a Sunday, but there are a lot of cars on the road. Bobby has to think about his driving on the two-hour drive from his little town, Powell, to the college in Brenton. But it's a beautiful September day, and soon he's feeling good. It's the first time for Bobby to live away from home. He smiles and thinks, *Brenton College, here I come!* He turns on the car radio and listens to some soft rock music.

The drive goes well for over an hour. The sun is coming in the car window as Bobby drives down the highway to Brenton. He looks at the trees and flowers near the road. *Brenton's big, not like Powell,* he thinks. *Powell has just 8,000 people. Maybe the other students are from the city, not from little towns like mine.* He thinks about Monday, too. His classes start tomorrow. What are the teachers like? What about the other students?

Then, near Brenton, Bobby sees a motorcycle behind him. *That's going fast,* he thinks as he looks behind him. It's a black motorcycle, and the rider is wearing a red jacket and has a red-and-white helmet on his head. He looks again. The motorcycle is right behind him now! Bobby looks at the rider: he's a young man, about Bobby's age. *Is he smiling?* Bobby thinks. *He looks like he's smiling.* Then, the motorcycle comes fast really near Bobby's car and then right in front of him. Bobby stops his car. He opens his window. "Hey!" he calls angrily to the man on the motorcycle. But the rider rides away.

Bobby is very angry. *What a crazy man!* he thinks. But he feels bad now and he drives slowly all the way to Brenton College.

◇◇◇

Bobby is still angry when he gets to Brenton College. He parks his car in the parking lot for Robert Adam House dorm, where his new room is. He walks to the dorm office to get his key.

"Room 213. Your roommate's there. Since Friday," says the man in the office, smiling at Bobby. "Any problems, you come and see me, OK?"

"Thanks," says Bobby. *He's friendly, anyway,* Bobby thinks. *I hope my roommate is nice too . . .*

As Bobby walks up to his room, he can hear very loud rock music. *Where's that coming from?* Then, as he gets near the door of Room 213 he can hear that the music is coming from his room! He looks at the number on the door again. *Is this the right room?* he thinks. But it is. Bobby opens the door and the music gets louder. The first thing he sees is a lot of clothes on the floor, a pizza box, and two or three soda cans. The second thing he sees is his roommate, smiling at him, wearing a red jacket, and with a red-and-white motorcycle helmet in his hand.

Chapter 2

Ash

"You!?"

Bobby's roommate smiles a big, open smile.

"I'm Ash," says the young man. "Ash Browning." He turns the music down and walks to Bobby, putting out his hand.

"Um, Bobby Harris," Bobby replies, taking his hand. *Hey, do you always ride your motorcycle that badly?* he wants to say, but he doesn't say anything. He just looks around the room. His face is serious.

Ash smiles. "It's just like home, isn't it?" he says. "We're going to have a great time, you and me!"

Ash is nice, and it's hard for Bobby not to smile. "Well," he says, "I need to get my things from the car."

Five minutes later, Bobby comes back with his things. He puts them on his bed and starts to put his clothes and other things away.

Ash comes over to Bobby and starts to help him. "Hey, what's that?" Ash asks. In his hand is one of Bobby's shirts, a brown one. "That's a really bad color . . ."

Bobby takes his shirt and gives Ash a bad look. But Ash doesn't stop. He takes another shirt, then some pants. Everything is brown or gray. "Ugh, Bobby," he says, "you have some really uncool things here. Why don't I help you look cool?" Ash is smiling all the time; it's hard for Bobby to get angry. Ash goes to his clothes and gets a white shirt. He puts it next to Bobby. "There!" he says. "It looks good on you!"

Bobby looks in the mirror and sees that Ash is right. The shirt does look good on him. "I don't think about clothes much," says Bobby.

Now Ash is right next to Bobby and looking at the photo of Bobby and his mom and dad.

"That's my mom and dad," Bobby says.

Ash doesn't reply. Bobby sees he's laughing.

"What is it?" Bobby asks.

"Nothing," Ash says.

"What? What's so funny?"

Is he laughing at my photo? Bobby thinks.

"Here give me that," Bobby says. He takes the photo and looks at it.

"I'm sorry, Bobby," says Ash. "It just looks funny."

Ash hits Bobby on the back again, and says, "Hey, there's a party this evening over at the girls' dorm. Why don't we go?"

"I don't know . . ." Bobby starts. Tomorrow is the first day at college. He has class at nine o'clock and he wants to have a good night's sleep.

"Come on, Bobby," says Ash. "It'll be great!"

"But we have classes starting tomorrow," Bobby says.

"Hey," says Ash. "Don't you want to meet some girls, too?"

"Well . . . yes," says Bobby. "OK, let's go."

"You can wear my shirt," says Ash.

Chapter 3

A bad day

The next morning, Bobby opens his eyes and looks at his clock. It's ten o'clock! He usually gets up at seven. He gets out of bed quickly.

Ash is still sleeping.

"Ash," says Bobby. "Come on, it's late."

Ash doesn't reply.

Bobby puts on a shirt and some pants. He takes another look at Ash, then he runs quickly out the door. Fifteen minutes later he is sitting in Dr. Lang's Business Studies class. He's trying not to sleep.

For about thirty minutes, Bobby tries to listen to Dr. Lang. His eyes start to close.

"Late night?"

Bobby opens his eyes to see Dr. Lang looking at him.

"Sorry?" Bobby says. "Um . . ."

"I said, 'Late night?'"

"Sorry, sorry," Bobby sits up, and Dr. Lang goes on with the class. After the class, Dr. Lang talks to him about it.

"Not a good start," says Dr. Lang. "Late on the first day and sleeping in class."

"No, sir," says Bobby. "I'm sorry . . . it . . . I . . ."

"Some students think business studies is easy. Is that what you think?" Dr. Lang asks him.

"No, I don't think that, Dr. Lang," Bobby replies. "I won't do it again."

Bobby goes out of the room. He's angry. *I'm so stupid!* he thinks. But he's sleepy all day. Ash doesn't come to class at all. Bobby thinks, *I can't go to parties and get up late. I have to study!*

◇◇◇

"Look at this, Bobby," says Ash, smiling.

Bobby is walking into his room after classes. He feels tired. Ash is there, sitting at his table and looking at his laptop computer.

"What?" asks Bobby.

"This video on the Internet," Ash replies. "It's *really* funny."

"You didn't go to class today," says Bobby. "Your first day!"

"Don't worry, Bobby. There's always tomorrow."

"And this room, Ash," says Bobby, looking around the messy room. "It's . . . as bad as yesterday."

"Stop worrying, Bobby. It's nothing," says Ash. He's smiling his big, open smile. "Here, come and see this."

Bobby sits down next to Ash and they watch the video. In it, a man is on a train, singing.

Ash starts to laugh. Bobby doesn't want to laugh, he wants to study, but it *is* funny.

"That's great," he says. "Look, I need to rest for a few moments."

"Wait. Here's another one for you."

Ash shows him another video. And another. An hour goes by.

Then, Bobby looks at his watch. Six o'clock!

"I have to go," he says and he gets up quickly.

"Go?" asks Ash. "Where?"

Bobby puts on his jacket. "The cafeteria," he says. "I'm working there evenings."

"Oh," says Ash. "Well, there's a party again tonight. When you finish, we . . ."

"No, Ash," says Bobby quickly. "I can't." *I'm here to work, to study,* he thinks, *not play around with computers or go to parties.* He goes out of his room and runs to the cafeteria.

Bobby goes in the door of the cafeteria and asks one of the workers for the manager, Gayle King.

"She's over there," says the worker. He looks at a woman in the door of the kitchen. "Go on, it's five minutes after six."

Bobby runs to Gayle. "I'm here, Ms. King," Bobby says to her. "Bobby Harris."

Gayle looks at her watch. "Mmm," she says. "This is not a good start. It's your first day and you're late. But come back in the kitchen and I can show you what to do."

Bobby goes into the kitchen and starts work. He feels very tired but he really tries to work hard. He does everything Gayle asks him to do. He helps in the kitchen and gives the students their dinner.

At nine o'clock, Bobby stops work. He eats something with the other workers and then he goes back to his room. He's very, very tired. He's happy to see that Ash isn't there.

Great—Ash is at the party, he thinks as he gets into bed. *Now I can get a good sleep . . .*

Chapter 4

A talk

"Wha . . . !" Bobby opens his eyes. From his bed, he sees Ash coming into their room.

"Sorry, Bobby," says Ash quietly.

Bobby doesn't speak. He looks at his watch next to his bed. Three-thirty! He waits for Ash to go to bed, then he tries to sleep again.

Five minutes go by. Then, "ZZZZZ, ZZZZZ." Bobby opens his eyes again. It's Ash! He's sleeping and snoring very loudly. In the night, Bobby tries to get to sleep again and again, but he can't.

◇◇◇

"Mr. Harris!"

It's Friday, the last day of Bobby's first week. Ash goes to parties and he's up late every night, and Bobby isn't sleeping well. Now Dr. Lang sees him sleeping in class again.

Bobby opens his eyes and sees that everyone in the class is looking at him. He feels really bad.

"I don't know what you're doing," says Dr. Lang after the class. "This is the second time, and it's only the start of your time at Brenton."

"I . . . er . . ."

"Do you want to fail your Business Studies class?" asks Dr. Lang. "Because that's what's going to happen . . ."

Bobby goes back to the dorm, thinking about Dr. Lang's words. *What can I do?* he thinks. When he gets to his room, he hears his phone ringing.

"Bobby?" It's his mother. Bobby doesn't want to speak to her right now, but he has to.

"How's everything?" she asks.

"Good, Mom."

"Your studies?"

"Oh, OK." Bobby feels bad that he can't really say anything to his mom.

"And what about your roommate? Is he nice?"

Bobby thinks about Ash getting in late, snoring all night, and not going to his class. "Oh, yes," says Bobby. "Really interesting."

Five minutes later, Bobby puts down his phone. *This is really bad,* he thinks. *It can't go on like this!*

Bobby goes to the dorm office at the front of Robert Adam House. The man with the keys is sitting at his desk. His name is Mr. Park.

"Hey there," Mr. Park says. "It's Bobby Harris, right?"

"That's right," Bobby says.

"I always remember student names," he says. "What can I do for you, Bobby Harris?"

"Um," starts Bobby, "I want to change rooms."

"Really? Why?" asks Mr. Park. "That's a nice room you have there."

"Well, it's a little noisy."

"Noisy? Well, where's the noise coming from? Another room, or . . ."

"No, inside the room," Bobby says.

"I see."

"And it's messy," Bobby goes on.

"Ah. I understand."

Mr. Park looks on his computer.

"I'm sorry, Bobby, but there are no other free rooms. Why don't you talk to your roommate?"

"I do talk to him, but it doesn't do any good."

"I'm sorry to hear that. I can write down what you say, but it's not good for Ash. It looks bad, and there may be trouble for him. I don't think you want that, do you?"

"I don't want to do that," says Bobby.

"OK," says Mr. Park. "Talk to him again, then."

◇◇◇

"Hey, I'm sorry," says Ash.

"The thing is, Ash, I can't sleep at night," Bobby says. "When you come in, you . . ."

"I know . . . look, I'm sorry, OK?"

"I can't fail, Ash," says Bobby, his face serious. "My mom and dad . . . they work really hard, you know?"

"It's OK," says Ash. "I understand, Bobby. Don't worry."

"Thanks, Ash," says Bobby. He looks at his watch. "I'm going to the cafeteria now."

Bobby feels happy as he goes to work. *Maybe things will be OK now,* he thinks.

But when Bobby gets back to his room later, Ash is there with Dwayne Williams and two other students from the dorm. They're all laughing and having a good time. Music is playing. The room is messy again with soda cans and pizza boxes.

Bobby looks at Ash, but Ash doesn't say anything. He and the others go on laughing.

Bobby takes off his jacket and sits on his bed. He tries to read but he can't. It's very noisy.

"Ash!" says Bobby. "I'm really tired . . ."

"Sure, Bobby. Come on," says Ash to Dwayne and the two other students. "Let's go to the common room."

They get up and leave Bobby. The common room is a big room where all the students can talk and listen to music. But the common room is near Bobby and Ash's room, and Bobby can hear Ash and Dwayne and the others laughing all night.

Chapter 5

An accident

"What are you doing?" Janine, one of the kitchen workers, calls to Bobby.

Bobby opens his eyes and sees hot oil all over the kitchen floor. *Aagh,* he thinks, *I was almost asleep!*

Janine and some of the other workers help Bobby, and they clean the floor quickly. "I'm sorry," Bobby says to the workers. But Gayle, the manager, sees it all and comes over to talk to Bobby.

"This is really very dangerous, Bobby," she says.

"I'm sorry, Ms. King. Really I am," Bobby says.

"Sorry's no good, Bobby," she replies. "That hot oil can easily hurt someone very badly."

Bobby looks very sad, and Gayle says, "Just don't do it again, Bobby."

Bobby goes back to his room. He walks quickly. *This is all because of Ash Browning,* he thinks. *I can't study. I almost lose my job. I have to talk to him again. I have to make him understand!*

Bobby opens the door of his room, but Ash isn't there. On the table he sees a note.

> Hi Bobby,
> I'm with Jenny. My motorcycle is broken so I have your car. Hope it's OK! See you later.
>
> *Ash*

"What?!" Bobby says. He looks for his car keys on the table, but they aren't there. He runs out of the door and goes into Dwayne's room.

Dwayne is on his bed, watching TV.

"Where is he?" Bobby asks.

"Hey, Bobby. Where's who?"

"Who do you think? Ash! He has my car!"

"Oh, yeah. His motorcycle is broken . . ."

"I don't care about his motorcycle!" says Bobby. "Where is he?"

"I think he's going to the lake."

"Can I take your bicycle?" asks Bobby. Dwayne has an old yellow bicycle that he rides around the college.

"Sure. Here's the key . . ."

Bobby doesn't listen anymore. He runs downstairs and gets on Dwayne's bicycle. He goes quickly to the lake. *My car, eh? That's too much! I'm really going to talk to you now, Ash Browning,* he thinks.

As he gets near the lake, Bobby can see Ash. He's with Jenny. *And there's my car,* he thinks. He cycles fast toward Ash. He's angry and he goes faster and faster. *Ash! You're making things so difficult for me!* he thinks. Bobby is so angry, he doesn't watch the road carefully. The bike hits something on the road. Bobby falls over the front of the bicycle and onto the ground.

"Aagh!"

Ash looks round. "Bobby?" he says. "What are you doing here?"

"Aagh! My arm . . ." Bobby replies.

◇◇◇

Ash and Jenny look at Bobby. Their faces are worried.

"Bobby!" Ash comes near him and looks at his roommate's face. "Bobby, what is it?" Ash's face is white.

Then Bobby's eyes open.

"What is it?" Jenny now asks.

Bobby doesn't speak.

"Come on," says Jenny. "Ash, get the car. Quickly. It's his arm." Ash drives the car to Jenny and Bobby. Then Jenny and Ash help Bobby to get up and into his car.

"I think my arm's broken," says Bobby.

"We need to go to the hospital in Brenton," says Jenny when they are in the car. "Come on, Ash. Drive!"

◇◇◇

"Well?" asks Jenny. Bobby is walking out of the Emergency Department at Brenton Hospital. Ash looks at his arm in a white plaster cast.

"It's broken," says Bobby. He looks at Ash. The three of them are in the waiting room of the hospital.

"Oh, that's too bad," says Ash.

This is too much for Bobby.

"Too bad?" he says. "Too bad?! You're the one that's too bad! You're making things very difficult for me, Ash! I can't sleep. I can't study. I can't work well. Now I can't do anything, because my arm is broken. And it's all because of you, Ash!"

"I . . ."

"You think you can do anything, don't you?" Bobby goes on. "Play music when you want. Put pizza boxes and clothes everywhere . . . Make noise all the time . . . Take people's cars without asking them . . . What about other people, Ash? You don't think about them at all, do you? And I don't even like pizza!"

Ash thinks about that.

"I can get Chinese food next time . . ." he says.

"Forget about the food, Ash!" Bobby goes on. "Can't you see? I can't work, I can't study. I can't do anything here . . . !" Bobby is very angry and he can't go on. He stops talking and looks at Ash.

The three of them are in the waiting room of the hospital. People are looking away, trying not to listen. Ash doesn't say anything for a minute.

Then he says, "You're right."

"What?" Bobby says.

"You're right. I'm really sorry, Bobby. I understand why you're angry. I'm stupid. Really stupid! But don't worry. This is me. This is my mess. And I can make it right. Don't worry about your job. Don't worry about your studies. Leave it to me, Bobby, I can help."

He puts his arm round Bobby.

"You watch, Bobby. I can make this right," Ash tells him.

"Careful with my arm," Bobby says.

"Sorry," Ash replies.

Chapter 6

Mom visits

"See you later, Bobby," Ash says, as he opens the door of their room.

It's a week later, and Bobby can't work because of his broken arm. Ash tells Bobby's manager, Gayle, and now Ash is working in the cafeteria for him.

"Thanks for doing the cafeteria job for me," says Bobby.

"It's no problem, Bobby," Ash says. "I can work there until your arm's OK, Gayle says. She says hi, too."

"And thanks for doing this." Bobby looks around their room. It's clean for the first time. There are no clothes or pizza on the floor.

"It's OK," says Ash, smiling his big, open smile. "You just study." And with that, he goes out.

Bobby goes back to his books. He's happy that he and Ash are friends again. He's happy that Ash is helping him. But most of all, he's happy about speaking to Ash, happy he's trying to make things right. He feels good about that.

Maybe we can be friends, he thinks.

Ten minutes later, his mother calls. "How are you, Bobby?" asks Gloria Harris. "How's the arm?"

"It's OK," says Bobby. "The doctor says my arm needs about two more weeks."

"Two weeks!" Mrs. Harris says. "I'm coming on Saturday morning to do some things for you. You need help . . ."

"It's OK, Mom . . . really . . ."

But Bobby's mom doesn't listen.

Bobby puts the phone down. He's worried. *Ash is doing well,* he thinks. *He's listening to me now, but can it go on? And what about Mom? It's going to be more difficult to make Mom listen!*

◇◇◇

"Mrs. Harris. Nice to meet you," says Ash, giving her a big, big smile.

It's Saturday morning, and Bobby's mother is at Brenton College to see her son. She's in Bobby and Ash's room. There are no pizza boxes or soda cans on the floor. The room is clean, and there are flowers on the table. Ash cleans the room every day now. At Ash's table there are open books.

"What a nice room," says Mrs. Harris. She smiles. "You boys are doing well."

"Thank you," says Ash before Bobby can speak.

"How are your business studies?" asks Mrs. Harris. "Are you studying hard, Bobby?"

"They're OK," says Bobby.

"Bobby's doing very well, Mrs. Harris," says Ash. "He's helping me, too. We study together. I think that helps a lot."

Bobby looks at Ash, his eyes big behind his glasses. *Is this really Ash?* he thinks. Then he looks at his mother. He can see that his mom likes Ash. She's smiling at him.

The three of them talk for some time. Then Bobby says, "Come on, Mom. Let me show you the college."

"What a nice boy, your roommate," says Bobby's mom to Bobby as they walk out of the dorm building. "I know I don't know him, but I can see he's a good boy. He works hard. He's a good student. You know, I think you can learn a lot from him, Bobby."

Bobby stops. He opens his mouth to speak. There are a thousand things he wants to say, but he can't remember what they are.

Review

A. Match the characters in the story to their descriptions.

1. _____ Bobby Harris
2. _____ Ash Browning
3. _____ Gloria Harris
4. _____ Gayle King
5. _____ Jenny Basola

a. manager of the Brenton College cafeteria
b. a new student at Brenton College
c. Bobby's mother
d. Bobby's new roommate
e. Ash's friend

B. Read each statement and circle whether it is true (T) or false (F).

1. Bobby has never lived away from home before.   T / F

2. Bobby's hometown is bigger than Brenton.   T / F

3. Ash thinks Bobby has nice clothes.   T / F

4. Bobby has to work in the evenings.   T / F

5. Ash is very worried about his studies.   T / F

6. Bobby complains to his mother about Ash.   T / F

7. Ash does not ask Bobby if he can use his car.   T / F

8. Bobby has a broken leg.   T / F

9. Ash keeps the room clean after the accident.   T / F

10. Bobby's father decides to visit him.   T / F

C. Choose the best answer for each question.

1. How does Bobby know Ash is the person on the motorcycle?

   a. He recognizes Ash's voice.

   b. He sees Ash's motorcycle outside.

   c. He recognizes Ash's jacket and helmet.

2. Which of the following is NOT a reason why Bobby can't sleep?

   a. Ash parties late every night.

   b. Ash studies late every night.

   c. Ash snores very loudly.

3. Bobby does not change rooms because _____ .

   a. he does not want Ash to look bad

   b. Ash asks him for another chance

   c. Mr. Park doesn't want to give him a new room

4. How does Bobby get to the lake?

   a. by car

   b. by bicycle

   c. by motorcycle

5. How does Ash help Bobby after the accident?

   a. He does Bobby's schoolwork.

   b. He shows Bobby's mother around.

   c. He takes over Bobby's job in the cafeteria.

D. Complete the crossword using the clues below.

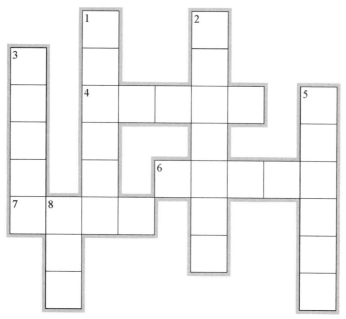

Across

4. Bobby's mother says he can _____ a lot from Ash.

6. Bobby watches a _____ with Ash and is late for work.

7. Ash leaves a _____ for Bobby about borrowing his car.

Down

1. Ash wears a _____ when he rides his motorcycle.

2. Bobby's mother is always _____ about something.

3. Bobby has a lot of _____ and gray clothes.

5. Ash _____ very loudly when he is sleeping.

8. Gayle King tells Bobby that hot _____ can hurt someone.

Background Reading:

Spotlight on ... *Getting Along with Your Roommate*

Starting college can make you really nervous! You will meet new people, study new subjects, and live in a new place. You will also have to learn how to live with a new person, your roommate. But this does not have to be difficult. Here are some tips:

1. Contact your roommate before classes begin.

Your college will most likely give you your roommate's contact information before classes begin. Call or email your roommate and ask what their hobbies and interests are. Show that you care about who they are and what they like.

2. Decide who should bring what.

By talking to your roommate early, you will get a chance to plan who brings what to the dorm. It would be funny if you both showed up with a TV! If you decide who will bring a small refrigerator and other items ahead of time, it will make it easier to move in.

3. Agree on the rules.

Your dorm room is a place where both you and your roommate will want to be happy living in. Come up with some rules that you both agree on, such as how clean you want your room to be, or whether visitors are allowed if one of you is studying.

Set some rules about keeping the room tidy!

4. Respect each other

Many people believe that they can get away with anything in college since they are no longer around their parents. But when you're sharing rooms with somebody, it is important that you respect each other's wishes. Don't be afraid to speak up if someone is disrespectful towards you. It happens to many people and it is important that you move on.

5. Have a positive attitude.

Your roommate will probably get on your nerves from time to time, no matter how many rules you agree on beforehand! Just remember to keep a smile on your face when things go wrong. Remember that your roommate is learning how to live in a new place just like you are.

Think About It

1. What are other things you can do to get along with your roommate?

2. Have you ever lived in a dorm with a roommate? What was it like?

Spotlight on ... *Friendship*

Friendship is born at that moment when one person says to another, "What! You too? I thought I was the only one."

Anon

The only way to have a friend is to be one.

Ralph Waldo Emerson

Good friends are good for your health.

Irwin Sarason

An old friend will help you move. A good friend will help you move a dead body.

Jim Hayes

Friends are needed both for joy and for sorrow.

Samuel Paterson

I don't need a friend who changes when I change and who nods when I nod; my shadow does that much better.

Pluto

Friends are those rare people who ask how you are and then wait to hear the answer.

Anon

A real friend is one who walks in when the rest of the world walks out.

Walter Winchell

> *A good friend can tell you what is the matter with you in a minute. He may not seem such a good friend after telling.*
>
> **Arthur Brisbane**

> *A true friend is someone who thinks that you are a good egg even though he knows that you are slightly cracked.*
>
> **Bernard Meltzer**

> *Am I not destroying my enemies when I make friends of them?*
>
> **Abraham Lincoln**

> *The most I can do for my friend is simply to be his friend.*
>
> **Henry David Thoreau**

> *Money can't buy friends, but you can get a better class of enemy.*
>
> **Spike Milligan**

Think About It

1. Which of the quotes do you like best? Why?

2. Make a list of 10 things you look for in a friend. What is the most important quality in a friend?

Glossary

age	(*n.*)	Your age is the number of years since you were born.
cafeteria	(*n.*)	a cheap student restaurant at a college
cast	(*n.*)	a covering used to protect and heal broken bones
clean	(*n., adj.*)	If a room is clean, it is not dirty and everything is in its right place.
cool/uncool	(*adj.*)	If something is (un)cool, it is (un) fashionable.
dorm	(*n.*)	A dorm (dormitory) is a building where many students live in a school or university.
fail	(*v.*)	If you fail a course, you did not study enough and you have to take it again.
funny	(*adj.*)	If something is funny, it makes you laugh.
helmet	(*n.*)	You wear a helmet on your head when you ride a motorcycle.
highway	(*n.*)	A highway is a wide road where cars go fast.
job	(*n.*)	Your job is the work you do for money.
lake	(*n.*)	A lake is a big area of water, often in a park.
mess (messy)	(*n., adj.*)	If a room is a mess (messy), everything is in the wrong place.
mirror	(*n.*)	You look in a mirror when you brush your hair.
noise (noisy)	(*n., adj.*)	A noise is a big sound—for example, a train station is noisy.
oil	(*n.*)	Oil is used to cook things like burgers and fries.
pain	(*n.*)	If you feel pain, you have hurt yourself, for example, if you fall off a bike.
party	(*n.*)	When many people meet, dance, have fun, and talk to friends, it's called a party.
ride (rider)	(*v., n.*)	When you get on a bike and move it, you are the rider and are riding it.
snore	(*v.*)	When you snore, you make a noise with your mouth while sleeping.
town	(*n.*)	A town is a place with a post office, houses, stores, and other buildings.

NOTES